# My Journey to Becoming a Mayan Shaman

Zachary Alexander Jezek

K & Z Enterprises
6822 - 22nd Ave N, Suite 345
St. Petersburg, FL 33710-3918

ISBN # 1-880534-15-0
Alexander Publications

**Credits & Acknowledgements**
Written by © Zachary Alexander Jezek, age 10
Edited by © Kytka Hilmar-Jezek, *www.ageofattraction.com*
Foreword by © Jeannine Parvati Baker
Photographs by © Kytka Hilmar-Jezek
Photograph of Rev. Dr. Dennis Alexander © Dennis Alexander
Circle & Shaman Ritual written by © Reverend Shaman Dennis
    Alexander, The Sentient Temple, *www.mayanreiki.com*
Layout by Sunny B. DiMartino

*Special thanks to my Aunt Kati and Uncle Joel Samon for giving us the space and funding to go back in this way in order to move forward. Thanks also to my mother for writing and editing this for me on the computer and for taking all of the pictures of me. To my father, for babysitting my sisters so that we could have the time needed to work on this. Family is the greatest blessing in our lives. To my Shamans; Dennis, his wife Fern and Kay for allowing me into the circle when they are not there and for helping me to see the power I have in my self.*

"Shamans are sometimes considered healers or doctors, but really they are people who deal with the tears and holes we create in the net of life, the damage that we all cause in our search for survival. In a sense, all of us - even the most untechnological, spiritual, and benign peoples - are constantly wrecking the world. The question is: how do we respond to that destruction? If we respond as we do in modern culture, by ignoring the spiritual debt that we create just by living, then that debt will come back to bite us, hard. But there are other ways to respond. One is to try to repay that debt by giving gifts of beauty and praise to the sacred, to the invisible world that gives us life. Shamans deal with the problems that arise when we forget the relationship that exists between us and the other world that feeds us, or when, for whatever reason, we don't feed the other world in return."

—Martin Prechtel

*"Educate the children to see with eyes of the future, standing firm in the present, on the strongest legs possible. Teach them the art of loving, the truth, the wisdom of the ages, with the simplicity reserved for those of innocence and with the tenacity of the sage."*

—Orion

# Foreword

*"From the simple opening sentence, I was captivated by this ten year old author. My Journey to Becoming a Mayan Shaman is a beautiful testimony to an enlightened home school and a glimpse into a free spirit's world. Throughout the read I thought to myself, if this boy went to school, how different a book he would write. For example, would he have been able to travel so extensively? Where would he have found the time to adorn his shaman's staff as his inspiration commanded? Would his profound message, 'I wish more children who are like me would be interested in healing instead of war and video games because what we learn and do today is who we will grow up to be tomorrow,' still be the same?*

*After reading Zachary's book, this may be every reader's wish as well -- the Earth needs a lot more Zachary's with his vision and devotion to actualizing what is best-for-life and for all our relations. I finished the book with deep gratitude to Zachary's parents for helping their son be all he can be. Out of the thousand feelings crowding my heart for Zachary, it is with full gratitude that I now say, 'Thank you Zachary,' for having wisely chosen your parents.*

*I recommend this book for all youngsters and those who are humble enough to keep learning from children. My teenager enjoyed the read and it brought out some memories from his own 'shamanic youth.' This is truly a book for all ages as now, being a grand mother, I will read it to my children's children. I look forward to reading many more reports from the new field of Reiki Maya Shamanism. Indeed I can hardly wait for any and all new books by Zachary Alexander Jezek."*

*Blessed Be & Blessed Do,*

*—Jeannine Parvati Baker*


Website: *http://www.freestone.org*
Author: Prenatal Yoga & Natural Birth, Hygieia: A Woman's Herbal
Co-Author: Conscious Conception with Frederick Baker
Co-Founder: Six Directions
Director: Hygieia College Mystery School in Woman Craft & Lay Midwifery

"There are more things in Heaven and earth, Horatio, than are dreamt of in your philosophy."

—Shakespeare, Hamlet, Act I

# Foreword from Zachary's Shaman

*"I have had the extreme pleasure of tutoring Zachary as an apprentice Shaman, during a period of two years. I found him so very attentive and serious for a young man of few years. Often students who are two or three times his age don't possess the zeal or desire to learn as Zachary does. When heard that he had written a book I wasn't surprised. A copy was left with me to read and I thought, 'Okay, I'll read this sometime soon.' Later, as I was getting ready to make a business call, and I had to move Zach's book to get to my address book. I flipped open his book to the first page and I was hooked!*

*My call didn't get made until after I had read the entire book. I have three published books in major books stores. This book deserves to be there along side of them. Zachary's work is outstanding, poignant and wonderfully entertaining besides being very enlightened. I feel as though I am blessed and that I and Kytka are molding a young Buddha.*

*I have walked the deep jungles of Honduras and lived with the Mayan peoples. I studied for three years to become a Shaman and after years of schooling to practice medicine I found the Mayan ways far reaching. When Zachary Alexander Jezek came to me and asked me to teach him my eye brow lifted. However I knew his mind was open, and he was not attached to the outcome of his Panche Be, Mayan for 'Seeking the Root of the Truth.'*

*I decided to teach him all that he could absorb at such a young age. The child/man astounded me! He further enlightened me when he handed me his book, 'My Journey to Becoming a Mayan Shaman.' I could not have been more pleased with his efforts. He was so complete in his thought processes. I increased his studies.*

*As I write this note, I am preparing him for his initiation in the sweat lodge in two days, once cleansed, he, on Sunday March 9th 2003, at the age of ten shall be ascended to Shaman. Zachary has earned this Honor. He shall continue to learn as I do each day. I believe the book will be re-titled as well it should be: 'My Journey to Becoming a Mayan Shaman.'"*

—Rev. Dr. Dennis Alexander, Shaman, Itzam K'in Balam X Manik

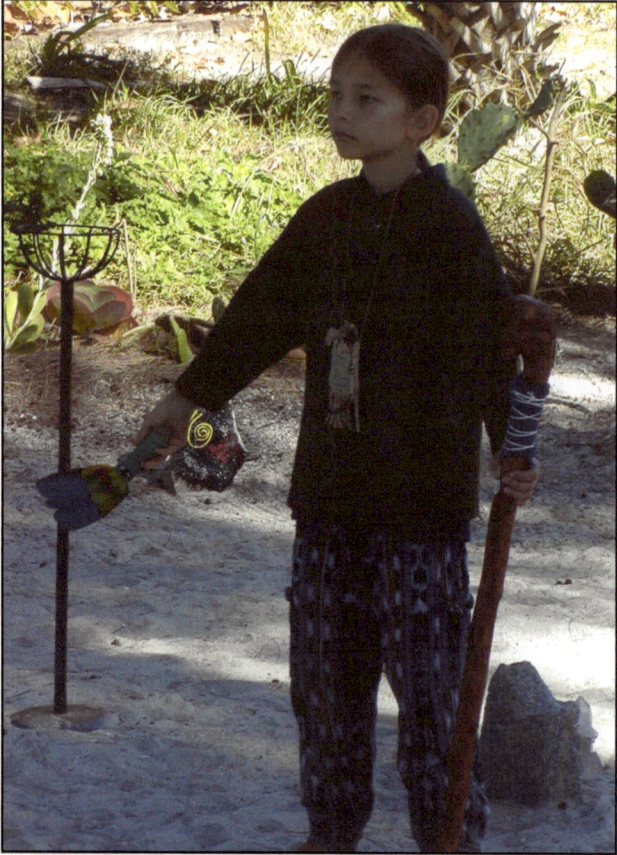

**M**y name is Zachary and I am ten years old. I am learning to be a Shaman. You do this by being an "Apprentice." This means that I am a Shaman in training.

I feel very lucky and blessed to have this honor, especially in today's times - when Shaman are not so easy to find.

My Shaman says that one does not learn to be a Shaman, but that one simply becomes a Shaman. It is something you are born with. I feel very lucky that I was born with it, and luckier still that I heard my calling!

Ever since I can remember, I wanted to be a helper and a healer. I want to take the pain away from the world. I want everyone to live in peace and to be without heartache and without sadness. I'd like to teach people to love each other and to be kind to each other.

When I was only 3 or 4 years old my favorite game was to play Doctor and Medicine Man. I remember driving through the desert and visiting the ruins in Arizona and feeling very safe and peaceful there in the quiet desert. My mother told me many stories about the healers of the past and how they have kept the people safe since the beginning of time.

My mother says that ever since we went there, I would take my play silks and dress up like the Native Americans of long ago. I didn't play warrior. I always played medicine man.

I like to collect feathers, sticks, stones and seeds and keep them in my special medicine pouch. I have collected these since I can remember and each new treasure I find speaks to me in some way and gives me a message or a feeling.

Some of my most powerful stones are from our visits to far away places. I have River Rocks from Oregon, lava rocks from Hawaii and a very old clay piece of pottery I found in Belize near a Temple ruin. I have some driftwood from Costa Rica and more from Washington State. My Shaman also gave me some maize (corn) and I carry it with me for protection.

I became very interested in Shamanism when I began to study Native Americans in my home school and I learned about medicine men.

My sisters and I were all born at home and my mother had midwives come to the births. My mom calls them wise women and when I asked if they were wise, she told me that they were like the medicine men I had been reading about. They helped my mom. They helped her to be strong and to trust her own power. I remember Mom laughing when I told her I wanted to be a "mid-husband" or a "mid-man"!

I too would like to help people to be strong and to find their own power. Helping people includes me using my Reiki. My mother taught me about Reiki healing and I am now a Reiki Master. First I learned all I needed to know about Level One. I learned about Dr. Usui and how he sat on the hill and the symbols showed themselves to him. Then I became attuned to Reiki Level Two. It was nice to get more symbols to work with. Finally the day came when I was Attuned to the Master Level. This means I can also teach and pass Attunements to others who want to practice Reiki.

It was hard to remember all of the chakras and the symbols at first, but the energy feeling was easy to feel right away. When my parents, my sisters or my animals feel sick, I want to help them to be better. Reiki showed me how to unblock the energy causing them the pain or sickness and how to try to move it out of their bodies. I like to be able to help people in this way.

I believe in Reiki and I have seen it working. When my grand-aunt came to visit me, she was very sick and in a lot of pain. She asked me to help her. I did and the very next day she called and said that she was feeling much better. She told me that her shoulder hurt, but I could feel sadness in her heart. I was kind to her and allowed the Reiki energy go where it needed to go. That is how the Reiki works.

Becoming a Shaman is a lot like having the Reiki power. I think maybe that the two are even the same - except that Reiki comes from Asian culture and Shamanism comes from the Americas. Shamans know about this power. They know how to ask for it and how to get it to flow through them. They use stones, dream visions and herbs to help too. There are medicine men and healers all over the world. These special people make it their life's work to help other people.

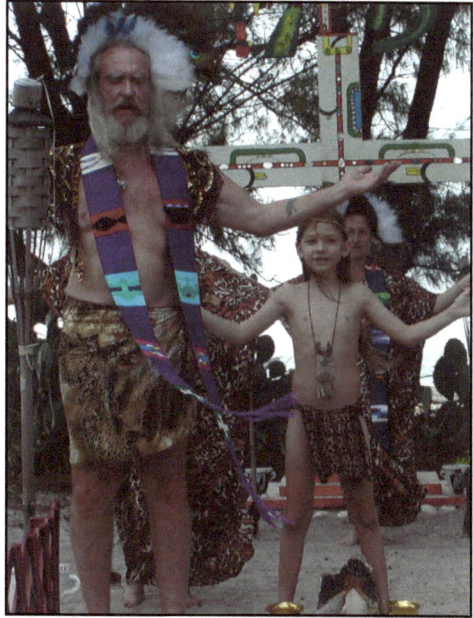

On my journey to becoming a Shaman, I worked on my own personal power, as well as understanding more the power of the universe to help and to heal others. This is what my Shaman does and what he taught me to do. My Shaman practices Mayanism and Mayan Reiki, which is a mixture of what he has learned from Reiki and from being a medicine man. He is a very good man who has helped many people.

My teacher on my journey is Mayan Shaman, K'in Balam XI Manik, Dennis Alexander. His name means SOLAR JAGUAR. He is also a Reiki Master teacher.

About 30 years ago he lived and worked in Honduras with the Mayan people. It was during this time that he became a Mayan Shaman through apprenticeship and ritual. He is known to the local people there as "Brujo Blanco," which means "White Witch Doctor." He did a lot of important work there and he helped many people. Now he helps people here!

Sometimes my Shaman travels to speak at conferences and to learn more. He knows Shaman from all over the world. He always has very special visitors at his house and in his circle. I like to be a part of this. I learn a lot from the other Shaman. A good student is a lifelong student because there is always more to learn. Even my Shaman learns from the visitors and he thanks them every time for coming and sharing their knowledge. I love to learn and am excited when the opportunity comes to gain more knowledge and experience and to meet other wise Shaman, especially from far away places.

*Mayan Shaman*
*K'in Balam XI Manik,*
*Dennis Alexander*

*Xunantunich*

I am very lucky in many ways. Last year, I got to go to Belize, Central America with my Shaman. We climbed to the top of an ancient Mayan Ruin called Xunantunich which means "stone woman" or "maiden of the rock." This was a ceremonial center with more than twenty five temples and palaces. This was also the first Mayan site to open to the public in Belize. It is a very beautiful and special place.

*El Castillo*

The largest pyramid there is called El Castillo and it rises a whole 130 feet above the main plaza!  That is a very long way to climb up with no railing and no safety net.  I was scared and I could feel my heart beating the whole way up but I felt I had to climb up.

When we reached the top we performed a ritual.  We spoke out to Hunab Ku, the giver of movement and measure.  I brought Copal incense which we offered to the Gods.  We stood there together for a very long time.  We spent this time just looking around and it seemed we could see forever because the day was so clear Looking within I could see that my place was here, learning to be a healer, a medicine man, a Shaman.  I was full of honor to be standing in this very special and powerful place with my Shaman/Teacher at my side.

This is the symbol for Hunab Ku. To the Mayan people he is the supreme God and creator of the Maya. They call him "God of the Gods." It is believed that Hunab Ku rebuilt the world after three terrible floods, which poured from the mouth of a sky serpent. The first world he created was inhabited by dwarfs, these were believed to be the builders of the cities. The second world he created was inhabited by the Dzolob folk. They were very mysterious and little is known about them. The third world which Hunab Ku created was created for the Mayan people themselves.

This is a glyph of Itzamna who is the son of Hunab Ku. Itzamna is known as "the Great God" or the "Lord of knowledge" because he taught the priests the art of scribe; writing. He brought the people maize and cacao and taught them all about healing and the use of calendars. Historians tell us that he brought culture to the people. He is also known as the Moon God; the one who rules over the night.

Glyphs are very fun to look at. They were the way the Mayan people wrote and recorded their history. The glyphs on stones and temples are like a history book that all the people of the village could read. When people visit the temples today, they can see the history all over the temples and stones. There is a great book my mother bought me called The Codex Borgia. This is a colorful book which shows many of the Mayan Gods, kings, warriors, mythical creatures, ceremonies, their calendar and so much more. It is fun to look for the many hidden meanings the Mayan people placed into the glyphs and to create your own glyphs.

My Shaman and I work in a circle. The circle is our sacred space. It is a place for ceremony, ritual and healing. Throughout all time circles have had great symbolic meaning in traditions all around the world. Circles are very powerful places. There have been many times when I have watched my Shaman touch people in the circle and I could feel their pain go away. I always feel the power in the circle, sometimes pulling me to the sacred tree. I really want to learn all that I can and I trust that everything my Shaman says is true. I know it is because I can feel it in my heart. He is a good man and I believe in what he teaches me. A good apprentice listens, watches and learns.

When we are in the circle, we light copal incense as an offering to the Gods, and to cleanse and purify ourselves and our space. It surrounds us and it smells so nice. We make offerings depending on the ritual we are having and who or what we are seeking to honor. Offerings can include herbs, flowers, corn, corn chips, blood, chocolate, honey, notes, wishes, pictures… anything.

I believe that when the items burn, the smoke carries the offerings to the Gods. The Gods like corn, chocolate and honey too. We burn them to represent the sweetness of life and to give thanks for all of our daily good fortunes. Mayan people believe that the more offerings are given, the more blessings are received into the world.

I am also learning to work with several tools. Shamans always use their tools to help them practice their medicine or healing. My Shaman gave me a special medicine pouch with my Mayan Day sign painted on it. My Day sign is OC, the symbol of a dog. My medicine pouch holds some sand from our circle and my most powerful crystals, stones and herbs. It also holds my special maize from Central America. My Shaman also gave me a head feather, which I wear in the circle. Later he gave me a conch shell and a wooden staff. All of these great things are my tools which I am learning to work with.

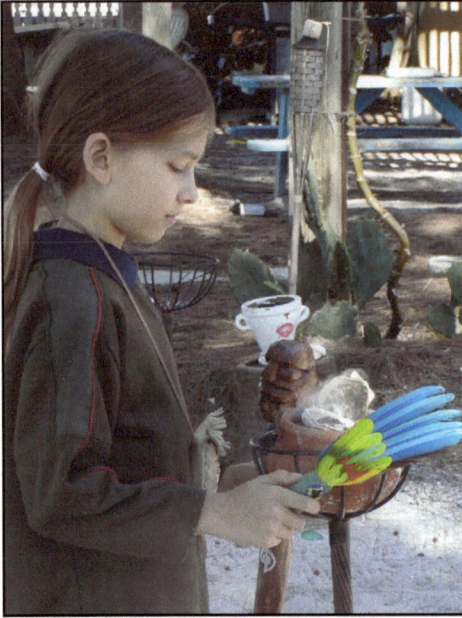

My mother gave me a beautiful feather fan with a very special crystal, which I use to smudge with. Smudging is when you cover something with smoke. This is done to cleanse and purify. You can smudge people, places, things... I also have some Reiki runes, a crystal pendulum and power animal stones. I have a very special place for all of these things and no one is allowed to touch them except me. They are my tools and I use them when I practice my Reiki and my Shaman's work. They are my sacred items.

Here is the Sacred Tree in the circle where I practice and learn. It is a beautiful and peaceful place by the sea. We can always hear the waves and I can feel the energy of the ocean. I am always barefoot in the circle and I can feel the energy of the earth as my feet sink into the sand.

One of my first times in the circle I placed my hand upon the sacred tree and it shook. It shook so hard I thought it would fall over! I could feel a pulling feeling. This made me shake inside and I knew right then that I was supposed to be working with this power. I knew I wanted to be a Shaman.

It took me a very long time but I have finally learned our sacred circle ritual. It is the one we say each time we visit the circle. We always begin and end in the same way. It is difficult because many of the words are in Mayan. It was hard to learn these new words and to remember them but it was important to address the Gods in their own language. My mother says that ancient languages hold a power of their own, and it was very important for me to learn the Mayan words.

This is what we say in our circle each time. It was written by my Shaman, Dennis Alexander.

We begin by holding hands and taking three breaths, then we chant, the God sound of manifestation three times; Ahhhhh. We follow this with the Ohm sound, three times.

Then we say the name of our Lord Sun, Ahau K'in three times; pronounced "AHH who keen."

Then we say the name of the Giver of Movement and Measure, Hunab Ku, three times; pronounced "uoo naa Koo."

Then we say the word of Peace, Shalome, three times; Shalome.

We pause and then face the East, our future. With one hand at our crown and one at our base chakra we say:

> *"From the Center of the Earth and the Center of the Universe, the Universal Life Force Ascending and Descending enters us, centers us, flows through us, empowers us; we become the conduits for the Universal Life Force. Tiox (tee oh she) Madre Munda (Mother Earth), Santa Mundo (Father Earth), and Nantat (Keeper of the Pool of Souls). Join us, Kukulcan (Koo Kool Caan), Chalchicutleque (Chall cheech oot lay coo ay) Tlaloc (Taa lock), guardians and guides, join us."*

Then we turn to the West, our ancestors and the Sacred Tree and we say:

> *"Uahomche, Uahomeche (Uoooa home cheee), We are within the tree and the Tree is within us. Xay tu pachan chul chan (Shay too paa chaan chool chaan), Cross roads of the sky Holy Heaven. Quice amo wa nuchac wa nupatan (Kee she amo wha new chak wha new paa taon), This is our work, this is our service."*

After this is said, my Shaman talks about whatever is happening that week. We send blessings and healing to friends and families of the circle and we send healing and love to the whole planet. When we are ready to close, my Shaman says:

> *"I place a Golden Matrix of protection around each and every person in this Circle and all those associated with it."*

Then he goes from person to person, and blesses them with the symbol of I'q. He draws a letter "T" on the forehead of each person and says:

> *"I'q is the the Breath of the Divine, and the Dai Ku Myo, The Tibetian Master Healing Symbol."*

Then he kisses each forehead to empower the symbols. Before we leave the circle we finish with; "We thank you for today, we thank you for yesterday and we thank you for tomorrow. So mote it be." This ends our circle and after this we usually have a reason to feast!

The "T" shaped symbol he makes on our foreheads is the symbol for the Mayan word I'q or Ik pronounced "eeek." It is the breath of life symbol which is the breath, the air, the spirit. Another way to say it would be "wind." It is drawn as a "T" because it forms half of a cross.

The Mayan people believe this represents the doorway into the spirit world. Many Mayan temples have windows and doorways shaped to a "T" because of this belief. This is a view from a temple at Palenque.

One of my heroes, the Mayan day keeper, artist, and historian named Hunbatz Men explains the meaning of this motif:

> "A transcendental synthesis of human religious experience
> is inherent in the word te, Sacred Tree, which emerged
> from the words teol and teotl the names of God the
> Creator in Mayan and Nahuatl. These most revered and
> sacred words of the ancient people, symbolized by the
> Sacred Tree, were represented in the Mayan hieroglyphs
> as the symbol 'T.' Additionally, this symbol represented
> the air, the wind, the divine breath of God." (1)

In other words, the T-shaped doorway or window symbolizes the Sacred Tree at the Center of the World (axis mundi) upon which the shaman's spirit may climb. In addition, it functions as the portal leading to the Great Spirit, through which the breath of life may pass.

One day my Shaman asked me if I was ready to lead the ritual. I told him that it would be a great honor. I practiced every night before I went to bed. I wanted it to be perfect when I did it. I wanted my Shaman to be proud of my efforts and to see how hard I had worked. I must be true to the power and remember that no matter how fun it is, that most of all it is sacred and to be used for a special purpose. My mother says a Shaman must have inner discipline and I try to work on that every day. My mother also teaches me the "code of ethics for the spiritual warrior." I use this every day along with the Reiki principles I learned.

I must always do and be my best. I must always remember to care for the other person. A Mayan Shaman is a man of service. I want to help and to serve. I want to be a good man like my Shaman.

Because my Shaman knew I wanted to practice I was allowed to go into the circle alone. I felt very connected to the power and to the Gods. I blessed my new feather fan and the new pendulum I received from my mother. I asked that my tools be filled with the powers of love and healing. I tried to say the whole ritual but I could not remember all of the words.

In my heart I could see myself saying all of the words with no mistakes. I could see myself holding my staff, decorated with feathers. I felt like I had seen the future.

After I left the circle, I felt like I needed to do something to show my Thanks for being there. I raked the sand in a careful spiral and I picked up all of the pine needles. This is also the work of the Shaman's Apprentice and the Shaman himself. The circle is a sacred place and it must be cared for.

In the beginning I was sad because I had trouble remembering all of the words but my mother told me not to be sad, that when I am ready, the words will come. That what I had seen in my heart would soon come to pass.

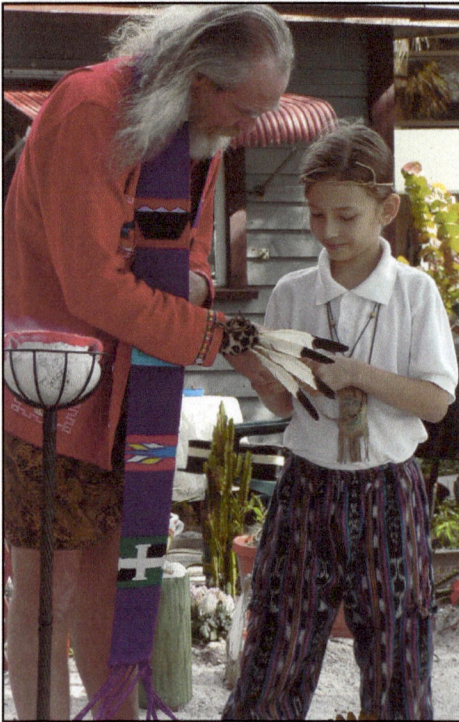

It felt good to honor the circle by taking care of it. Time passed and I became very good at the words just as my mother had said. My Shaman said that one must have patience and persistence. He also taught me that whatever you think can happen, can. He said that everything we see, everything we do and everything we are is thought manifested. That means that we think about something and then it becomes. This is true because I thought I would be able to become a Shaman one day and now I am one.

I have visions and thoughts all of the time. Some friends just call them fantasies or wishes, but I know about their power. Once I had a vision about standing in the circle holding my Shaman's staff. I went home and I began to work on my staff. I wanted very much for it to look like it had in my vision. My father helped me to add some feathers and leather wrapping to it. We worked on it all afternoon and then I worked on it some more. I worked on it until it felt right. My father also helped me to carve some wooden blocks onto which we carved some Reiki symbols. Later that evening what I had seen in my vision had come to pass. I was standing in the circle holding my Shaman's staff.

I use Reiki a lot too. Reiki teaches us not to worry or be angry. These are things which only harm us and block the goodness we have within us. My mother wanted me to learn about Reiki and so she wrote a book, Reiki for Children, just for me. She was sad that there were no Reiki books for children and she thought there should be one. Now there is! Her vision's come to pass too!

I think it is very important for me to do both Reiki and the Shamans work. I want to be like my Shaman. I want to practice what he calls Mayan Reiki. It is a combination of the best of both and I like the way it feels.

The day came when my Shaman felt I was ready for much more than holding a medicine pouch cleaning and sweeping around the circle. Each day I received more and more responsibilities. It was a lot of work and preparation. I had to study hard and practice all I had learned. My Shaman asked me to lead the circle many times. Each time my voice became more clear, stronger and louder. I attended memorial services and consoled people who had lost their loved ones. I welcomed new Reiki Masters into the group. I was present at many very important rituals and ceremonies. I met very important people.

Zachary Alexander Jezek

Then came the day when my Shaman announced I was to do a sweat lodge purification with him.  My Shaman told many stories of his sweats with the Mayans and the Apaches and I was afraid.  He said many grown men would faint or lose their breath.  He said many men could not endure the heat.  I tried with all of my might to remember the Reiki principles and not to worry.

My Shaman prepared me with a special protection ritual.  He also announced that I was to receive my Mayan name.

He drew the symbol of I'q in the most scared pollen, cattail pollen on my forehead for protection and to open my third eye.  This was a very exciting moment.  He spoke very slowly and described what the name meant and why he chose it for me and then he said it.  Buch Cho, pronounced Boosh-sho.  It means "smoke mouse."

He said mouse is very strong and can endure much; long journeys with little water, bad weather and hunger.  He also said that mouse can hear very well and that they always know when to enter a room.  Mice can sense when an enemy approaches and mice can smell danger in the air.  I was to think about my name and its meaning while in the lodge.

In Mayan, a sweat lodge is called a Tuj.  It is a very holy place, much like a church.  It is a place of prayer and a place of healing.  It is the place where we re-enter the womb of our mother, the earth.  When we come out, it is as if we are reborn.  We come out as "new."  Our identity changes and we are born again into a new identity.  I understood that I was going into the lodge as Zachary and I was expected to come out as Buch Cho.

My Shaman then placed his Golden Matrix over me and we went into the lodge.  It was very dark.  It was very quiet.  It felt very safe. I could smell the sage water which he slowly sprinkled over the hot burning river stones.  It smelled so good, my fear went away immediately.  He began to beat his drum and I listened.  The sound was rhythmic.  It was like my heartbeat.  It felt like my heartbeat and the heartbeat of the universe were one.

I thought about my name and as it got hotter and hotter I could see myself as Buch Cho, Smoke Mouse. I will be strong and endure as mouse does. I will be aware and look for the danger in the air. I will listen with my entire being....

As it got hotter and hotter, my vision of myself as Buch Cho became stronger. I saw myself as a powerful healer. I saw myself as a Shaman. All of my fears were replaced with a vision of me standing tall and proud as a Shaman.

I came out of the sweat lodge really feeling like I was new. Even the way I moved, I was like a mouse. I had to crawl out on all fours and my nose quickly caught all of the smells of the outside world. My ears immediately heard all of the sounds; the people on the beach, cars on the street in the distance. I had changed. I WAS Buch Cho.

It was overwhelming and I felt like much of it was a dream. Was I really so strong that I made it through the sweat lodge? Yes. I was. I made it. My Shaman was proud of me as were my mother and father. I was also very proud of my-self. I had been learning so much and now I passed this important test. I was on my way to becoming a true Shaman. This was an important day for me. It was a rite of passage and I am happy I went through it. I feel more comfortable in my changing body and in my new self.

My Shaman also taught me to practice Sufi. Sufi is a form of spinning which brings on a very clear mind. You spin counterclockwise in the direction of the rotation of the earth. Your right hand is pointed down to pull the energy up from the earth and your left hand is pointed up to release the energy. Sufi is a form of sacred dance. Mayan Lords and Leaders would dance on top of their temple pyramids in communication with the Gods. My Shaman told me that performing sacred dance raises very powerful energies, especially when you practice with others. It is best to do Sufi when your stomach is empty though because all of the spinning may make you sick if you are not prepared!

My Shaman has taught me so much about so many things. Being a Shaman is not only about medicine and healing. It is about being a good listener and about being able to love people even when they are angry at you or if they do not like you. This is called "Panache Be" in Mayan. It means "Seeking the root of the truth." My Shaman said it really means to see behind what is in front of you. He said that many people who are hateful or angry are really in a great deal of pain. Being a good Shaman means to be able to love even these people, because these people need your love the most.

Anger and hatred are like masks people wear when they are afraid to show their true selves. They are afraid people will think they are weak, or mistaken. They are afraid of what others may think. A Shaman does not judge people. A good Shaman loves and accepts everyone.

The day came when my Shaman announced that we would be having a very special ceremony. I believed it was because we were moving to Central America and that it would be like a going away ceremony. I saw that my Shaman had his fanciest ceremonial head dress out. This day was to be very special. I was very excited, but also very sad because I believed this was to be our last circle.

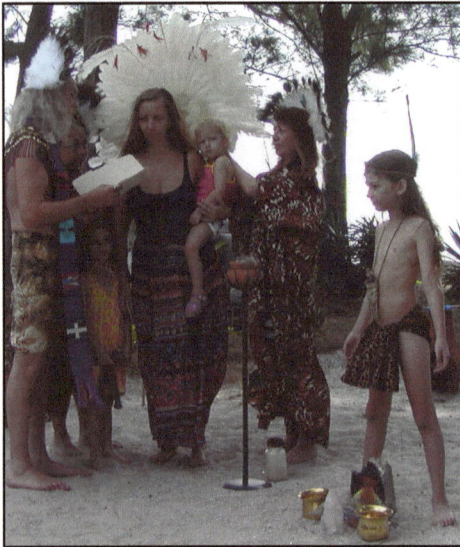

Right away it was different because I was told to wear my loin cloth and to walk into the circle last. Usually, I was one of the first ones into the circle and oftentimes I am the one who smudges the others. It was very strange to have to wait until everyone else was in the circle. I didn't understand and I had no idea what was going on.

I also noticed that my Shaman was very emotional. Usually his voice was very strong, but today his voice was quiet. I knew he would miss me as much as I was going to miss him. He had grown very close to me and he was like my best friend, my grandfather, my teacher and my guide all in one.

He brought out the ceremonial head dress and it was placed over my mothers head. He realized how much knowledge my mother had and how much time she had invested in working so much with me. He named her Buch Balam, Smoke Jaguar, and named her Honorary Shaman. My mother deserves it, she is very strong and smart. She helps everyone and is very giving and caring. I was so happy for my mother.

Then my Shaman began to speak and to say things I had never heard in our circle before. My mother stepped aside and the ceremonial head dress was placed over my head. I was being made a Shaman today! I could hardly believe it.

First my Shaman ordained me as a Minister of Ancient Ways. This would allow me to be able to practice my Shamanism wherever I would go. Then he began:

*"Xay tu pa chan – Cross roads of the sky – Ch' ul Chan – Holy Heaven, Wa' canmic quinjach wa' quipatan, This day I hand over your service…"* There was much more said, but I want to honor the sacredness of the ceremony and not share the rest. He then made me repeat after him: *"I receive my work, I receive my service"* and I was designated as a Shaman.

My Shaman and I both cried tears of joy.

I received many gifts from the other Shaman and members of the circle as they welcomed me into service. I received red clover as my herb, and dill flower essence to keep me calm and bring me into deep meditation. I received a Sastun which is my guide stone to healing, seeing and feeling.

I received my Shaman's amulet carved in jade, which will open my mind and my heart to my guides. I received my Astolie, which is much like a Priest's robe. Wearing it designates me as a Shaman in our circle and I received my Itzan Yeh as my crown. This special head dress is the symbol of my station as a Shaman.

I went in to the circle this day as Zachary and I walked out along the Shaman's path as Buch Cho, Mayan Shaman.

I am now a real Shaman. I have a great responsibility to myself and to others. I will honor my station and my position and I vow to go forth with love. The Journey was easy in many ways, but also difficult as is much in life. I learned so much along the way and I am proud of the special people who helped me and honored to be a part of their lives.

As I end this I would like to add a special message to the children who read this and also to mention some of the good books my mother has shared with to me which helped me on my journey and may help others on their journey to becoming a Shaman or just learning more about this way of life.

My special message to all children:

> *Trust in yourself and in your own power. Stay close to
> what your feelings tell you and don't do anything that
> doesn't feel right. Open your mind to things unusual
> and uncommon. Don't follow the crowd, they will lead
> you to nothing. Be proud to be different. Different
> people make a difference in the world.*
>
> *I wish more children would be interested in healing
> instead of war and video games because what we
> learn and do today is who we will grow up to be tomorrow.
> I also wish I had more friends who want to be healers
> and Shaman. Just think if we all had plans for a better
> world. Being a Reiki healer and a Shaman is not only
> cool and fun but also very important.*
>
> *I am doing something now because I want to be a
> responsible grown up living in a peaceful world. We
> will need many more healers in the future times if the
> world keeps polluting and wasting and poisoning like it
> does now. I want to grow up in a clean and safe world,
> in a world where we help each other and care for each
> other. How will we do this if no one is learning how?*
>
> *Be different.*
>
> *Learn about things like Reiki and Shamanism and
> practice every day like I do….*
>
> *Dare to make a difference!*

Zachary

# *Blessings and Peace*
# *to you all!*

# Afterword

I begin by saying that so much has changed, yet nothing at all.

I'm Zack and I am sixteen now. Looking back I see so much change in my life, going from Reiki, to Shaman apprentice, to Master and then ascending to Mayan Shamanism, everything giving me some of the best memories.

I still practice the art of healing and meditation, it is just that now I have found new things to work on and have added - such as the law of attraction which is very exiting! It is a little different because instead of healing one person at a time I have the power to both heal myself and the world. I am very grateful to all of the experiences that I have had for they have made me a much better person.

Just a year ago, I had an accident falling on my head which rendered me unconscious. My mother took me to the hospital and they found that I had a very unique temporal bone fracture. This is the accident that people get when they jump out of an airplane and their parachute fails to open. It is a deep bone within the skull that is very difficult to break.

At the time, we were in Costa Rica and the doctors there had not seen anything like that before, so they didn't know what to do. My mom was very scared and I assured her that I was going to be alright. Together we manifested meeting one of the very best Doctors in the world who specifically specializes in these types of injuries, in Costa Rica! In three weeks, I was good as new and back on my skateboard.

But the near death experience has added another element into my life. Now I am more conscious of living my life to the fullest, and in the "now."

These days, I am into skateboarding, art, music, writing, and I would like to thank my mother for all of her support, for she has helped me along the way by being so supportive and trusting of me and my dreams.

I try and inspire all of the people I meet along my journey. I ask that they try to be more like myself and enjoy what they have for it can, now, because it can all be taken away in a second. One never knows! So my words to share now are - bless your every day, for you have the gift of your life. Bless those in your life, for they have a purpose to be there and bless the world you live in, for it has given you so much.

I get so sad to see children and adults wasting their lives on things that don't even matter, small things that are all just passing, thoughts and emotions which seem to clog them down and shadow their brilliance.

I have always wanted to make a difference in this world and I never stop trying. I hope this book will inspire you to become more true to yourself and the world around you. I hope that it will show you that no matter how young or old you are, never give up, never stop healing the universe for it loves you…

Love it back.

# Kudos & Reviews

*"Ten year old Zachary Alexander Jezek presents children and their parents with an excellent introduction on becoming a Shaman. My Journey to Becoming A Mayan Shaman is very well written and an easy read.*

*This book includes beautiful photographs of Zachary learning and practicing to become a Shaman in his circle, a beautiful and peaceful place by the sea. What makes this book different from others is the sense one gets of the enthusiasm and self confidence of such a free spirit.*

*Zachary tells us stories from his own personal journeys to Arizona, Oregon, Hawaii, Costa Rica, Belize and his work with his Shaman. Zachary details his experiences with pride and innocence. His journey, since he can remember, has always been to help and heal others and the world. It is evident that he was truly born with a gift.*

*In his final message, Zachary gives kids practical advice on peace, believing in yourself and doing what feels right. I feel this message is a very powerful one with a strong and positive vision for other children to learn from. This book is a must read for anyone interested in Shamanism, Reiki, Indigo or Crystal Children, or even just for inspiration."*

*—Kati Samon*
*Mother and Teacher*
*BA Elementary Education*

▲ ▲ ▲

*"As America goes into the future, she faces real challenges as to the type of education and society that she exposes to her children. The separation of church and state is an important and fundamental difference between our culture and some of those around the world. This difference is very real and is something that should be understood by everyone in our society.*

*However, banning the teaching of the variety of religions that are found in our world does nothing to advance our 'civilization.' Forcing both parents to work, limits the contact children have with their parents and breeds a growing plethora of youth that struggles with how to* participate in a productive work force. Scaring parents into thinking that home schooling and breast feeding are somehow crimes against humanity is complete nonsense. And yet, this is the great empire we find ourselves in today.

For someone to challenge that status quo takes great courage and to see the fruit of that strength in the words of Zachary Jezek is a marvel. In all honesty, as I was reading his book, I could just hear the shrieks of the ignorant masses cringing at the word 'gods.' 'How unacceptable!' 'How regressionist!' 'How ungodlike!' Yet, after recently 'reading' Huston Smith's voluminous 'Religions of the World,' it seems quite clear that, to this day, there continue to be as many arguments for one God, as there are for twenty, or even none.

Zachary's book shows a great respect for culture, knowledge, and life. For anyone to think otherwise, only shows the limit of their understanding. There is a great, wide, wonderful world out there for everyone to participate in, and, though there are of course many aspects that should be questioned, at the same time, it seems to me that America should respect, investigate and possibly embrace some the new (if not old) ideas that other cultures offer. Should it really be a crime for a woman to stay home with her children? Or to teach them? Or to nurse them?

Science teaches us great insights into this tactile world we live in, but there continue to be even greater truths and secrets beyond our scientific reach, and until our species loses it's dominant hold on this planet (as have all other species that ruled before us), it will continue to be only those few that look deep within that can offer us a glimpse at the untouchable and unseeable miracles in this universe. Zachary Jezek pursues that calling."

—Scott Kissack
Learning Tree International

▲ ▲ ▲

*You are indeed a blessed young man to have found your path so early in life. I have shared your book with several children aged 5-11 and they all felt a connection to you. My 22 month old also enjoyed listening and looking at the photographs. I liked your book and appreciated the obvious respect you have for your teachers and your lessons. I would have liked to have known your interpretation of the purpose of the circle. Good luck on your journey. You will make a wonderful Shaman, Reiki Master and "mid-husband"!*

*Namaste*
*—Annette*

# Recommended Reading

*2012: The Return of Quetzalcoatl* by Daniel Pinchbeck

*Animal Speak: The Spiritual and Magical Powers of Creatures Great and Small* by Ted Andrews

*Boy into Man: A Father's Guide to Initiation of Teenage Sons* by Bernhard Weiner

*Breaking Open the Head: A Psychedelic Journey into the Heart of Contemporary Shamanism* by Daniel Pinchbeck

*Celebrating the Great Mother: A Handbook of Earth Honoring Activities for Parents and Children* by Cait Johnson and Maura D. Shaw

*Chosen by the Spirits: Following Your Shamanic Calling* by Sarangerel

*Crystals R for Kids* by Leia A. Stinnett

*Dark Night, Early Dawn: Steps to a Deep Ecology of Mind* by Christopher M. Bache

*Enlivening the Chakra of the Heart* by Florin Lowndes

*How to Make the World a better Place: A Beginner's Guide to Doing Good* by John Hollender

*Keeping a Nature Journal: Discover a Whole New way to see the World Around You* by Clare Walker Leslie & Charles E. Roth

*Maya Cosmos: Three Thousand Years on the Shaman's Path* by David Freidel, Linda Schele & Joy Parker

*Mayanism: A New Look at an Old Religion* by my Shaman, Dennis Alexander

*Medicine Grove: A Shamanic Herbal* by Loren Cruden

*Nature Spirits & Elemental Beings* by Margo Pogacnik

*Reiki for Children: Using Healing Touch and Raw Foods to Tap into the Power of the Universe* by my mother, Kytka Hilmar-Jezek

*Return to Creation: A Survival Manual for Native and Natural Peoples* by Medicine Story

*Sastun* by Rosita Arvigo with Nadine Epstein

*Shamanic Experience: A Practical Guide to Psychic Powers* by Kenneth Meadows

*Stories of the Spirit, Stories of the Heart: Parables of the Spiritual Path from Around the World* by Christina Feldman and Jack Kornfield

*The Fourfold Way: Walking the Paths of the Warrior, Teacher, Healer and Visionary* by Angeles Arrien

*The Thundering Years: Rituals and Sacred Wisdom for Teens* by Julie Tallard Johnson

*The Way of the Shaman* by Michael Harner

*Walking the World in Wonder: A Children's Herbal* by Ellen Evert Hopman

Daniel Pinchbeck speaks of 2012 and the end of time...

> *"Queztalcoatl represents the union of spirit and matter."*
> He proposes that the completion of the Great Cycle of
> the Mayan calendar and Queztalcoatl's return, due to
> take place in 2012, are archetypes.

> *"Their underlying meaning points toward a shift in the*
> *nature of the psyche. If this theory is correct, the*
> *transformation of our consciousness will lead to the*
> *rapid creation, development and dissemination of new*
> *institutions and social structures, corresponding to*
> *our new level of mind. From the limits of our current*
> *chaotic and uneasy circumstances, this process may*
> *well resemble an advance toward a harmonic, perhaps*
> *even utopian, situation of the Earth."*

Go forth in love....

# Recommended Web Sites

Zachary invites you to visit the following web sites:

My Site: *www.youngshaman.com*
My Teen Sites: *www.teensuccessbuilder.com* and *www.tapintoteen-power.com*

Our Reiki for Children Site : *www.reikikids.com*
Our Home School Site: *www.waldorfhomeschoolers.com*

Mom's Blog: *http://waldorf-spiritual-kids.blogspot.com/*
Mom's Site: *www.ageofattraction.com*
Mom's Book: *www.thegreatestwork.com*
Mom's DVD/Book: *www.raisingkidsraw.com*

My Shaman's Site: *www.mayanreiki.com*
My Shaman's Medical Qigong: *www.medicalqigongflorida.com*

My Favorite Mayan Site: *www.mayankids.com*

# Dream Notes

# Dream Notes

# Dream Notes

# Dream Notes

# Dream Notes

*Learning to live in the present moment is part of the path of joy.*

*–Sarah Ban Breathnach*

www.ingramcontent.com/pod-product-compliance
Lightning Source LLC
Chambersburg PA
CBHW041359090426
42741CB00001B/21